I

II

# INTERPERSONAL PROBLEMS?

# A THERAPIST'S HANDBOOK

## SOME SIMPLE TOOLS

**PUBLISHED BY**
**Gilles M. K. Desmarais M.D.**

**Library of Congress Cataloging-in-Publication Data**
**Desmarais, Gilles M. K., M.D.**

**Interpersonal Problems? A Therapist's Handbook**
**Some Simple Tools**

# CONTENTS

**I**

Eight Self-Help Tools

**II**

Feuding Personalities?

**III**

Unveiling Personality Behaviors

**IV**

In Control Of Dialogue

**V**

Education

**VI**

Dating

**VII**

Husband-Wife Significant Other
Negotiations

**VIII**

Learning About Children
or
How Did I Get Myself Into This Mess?

**IX**

The Quicksand Of Adolescence

**X**

Work-You & The Boss

**XI**

Tools For The Future

# PREFACE

This is a short book intended to make it simple for you to finish rather quickly. I'll give you a *set of tools* so that you can really understand what's going on with the people around you, which should lead to less anxiety and more enjoyment. You are probably encountering some problems at this time. You definitely will encounter more. It's good to be prepared just in case.

This book will help you to make better decisions when facing the problems of everyday life. That doesn't look easy at first glance, but when you look at the limited number of factors that are involved, it really is a lot easier than you think. This book will give you the tools to effectively do that by understanding the underlying causes of the problems. It will not be limited to one man's opinion or just one way of doing things. Self-help books tend to be "one size fits all" in their approach based upon personal experience. "One size does not fit all," there are always a variety of options. With that you will be able to evaluate the situation pretty clearly and make your decisions based upon reasonable options. After evaluating over 50,000 people over a span of forty years, this psychiatrist has been able to make a lot of observations and form his own set of conclusions about human behaviors. Our understanding of how the mind works is in its infancy. The researchers are working very hard to understand the biochemistry of the mind, but that's proving to be very complex and rather elusive. To be able to alter and improve people's behaviors it is absolutely essential to understand the root causes. So we are left with this piece of advice, "deal in the area that you know something about, do what you can, and accept your limitations. Don't act as if you have all the answers." A highly trained child/adolescent psychiatrist gave me this piece of advice, "There are six different ways of treating these children, pick which one seems to be the best, continue that for six months, then go to your second best choice, go down the line and things are bound to change. They're bound to grow up." Follow that with the economic term *ceteris paribus, a*ll things being equal, and they're never equal... so we're dealing in a fuzzy area. Let's do our best.

We know that emotions and logic compete for the same behavioral pathways. People are probably born with a certain personality structure and it is very hard to change that. We know that children born and raised by the same parents are often quite different people. Every individual has to cope with problems and issues at every stage of his

IX

life. The challenges change. One hopes the individual can conclude each stage successfully, click the *save* button and move on to the next stage, hopefully at a higher plateau. There are challenging issues at every stage. We all see rather blatant problems in marriages, in the raising of children and just getting along with the people that we encounter. One thing is quite clear... we are all naturally self-serving and self-centered. Nothing wrong with that. Many people are good actors, others are not. Many people are not aware that their friends, family and bosses see them as quite different people. We are all naturally quite self-defensive. Even the most intelligent, well schooled and experienced people still have their blind spots and trouble coping with things. Some see conflicts everywhere.

**You need to be in charge** of every role that you're playing in life. We all feel personal frustrations, most people recognize that they have limitations and try to do their best. But what is "the best?" So we are advised to turn to **experts** who probably should be best able to give us some direction. However, we have seen two experts repeatedly come to opposite conclusions. How could that be? Hopefully the information in this book will help to clarify. What is true of an expert is that he usually knows more about his field than we do. We have all heard of common sense and that probably plays a role. The Walt Street Journal found that someone simply throwing darts at the board did at least as well as the investment counselors! Ain't that something! So I'm going to list a number of problems that you will encounter, look at the factors that are involved, give you some reasonable information that would allow you to use some common sense options towards some resolution. Remember that a very good possible solution may not be possible. But if you understand that, **you are in control**. If the underlying causes of the problem is clearly understood, then you can deal with it, and not have that awful feeling of being overwhelmed.

# INTRODUCTION

The information that you receive in this book will really be of help to you, even if you are very bright and very intellectual and very well-rounded. It will cover many areas, many of which you encounter on a daily basis, and add pertinent information which may help you to reconsider your view of things or your actions. This is intended to be a good-natured book which you won't find offensive. It will probably benefit you, your family, your friends and your performance at work if you, unfortunately, are not a member of the idle rich. If you are not employed, but a significant other is, it will also probably help to enhance his or her performance. Should you be a member of the idle rich, this book would serve you well by offering you a better understanding of the behaviors of the people in your milieu. And in a **sinister** fashion, it might even help you to manipulate your environment. Gosh!, did I say that?

Remember, **you do need to be in charge**, in charge of the role that you are playing. That doesn't mean that you're the boss. If you are in school, then you have the role of a student and you need to be as effective as you can be. In calculus they use **max/min** and you can use that as a guide to your dedication and performance. We often "go with the flow" when we could alter the course of that stream. We can look back at our natural physical and mental endowments, and place that in the nurturance or unnurturance during our formative years. That impacts upon our expectations and potentials as we deal with the challenges of our lives. It's clear that the more knowledge that you develop by yourself, coupled with your experiences, will give you the information to use **critical thinking** when you are facing challenges. This book will ask you to ask yourself if you are coping with an issue from preconceived ideas and only demonstrating a reflex action... just being emotional. You can certainly be emotional over trivial things on a daily basis. Everybody does that. But where things really count you have to become more logical and do some critical thinking so that you can deal with it realistically. Then you can review your options...**max/min**. Many of our problems are rooted in our personalities and our preconceptions and expectations. You may be facing a wall with a different personality structure, different preconceptions and expectations. **Sound the clarion...call to arms!**

We will be going over an average range of personalities. You can decide what you are like to begin with. If you face personality issues, you need to understand how the other person is thinking. The reason "**why**" he thinks that way will probably not be of any value, although we would like to think so. "I wish it weren't so," but it is. You have to begin to deal with things in that way. The rest comes pretty easily. Then you, not me, have to factor in the intellectual factors, the physical factors and the individual preferences and dislikes, such as liking sports or music... or hating them. We'll be talking about that in more detail. Then there is the flexibility factor...are you, and the other people that you are interacting with, open to new ideas or priorities? We'll be discussing whether you are coming to the table with fixed ideas and automatically laying the problem onto somebody else's lap. It's extremely difficult for people to admit that the problem may be on their side of the table. That goes both ways of course. Is it in your best interests to be involved in a one-sided relationship in which the other person, or yourself, has to make the decisions all the time? We'll deal with problems with spouses, significant others, family, parents, bosses, finances... and a lot more... did I forget sex?

# PROLOGUE

So we'll start with the **personality package** = (IQ + physical traits + **personality**) x nurturance x knowledge x experience x **f (n+/n-)** x **d (d+/d-)**. **The f factor** is a key factor and refers to **flexibility**. The **d** refers to **determination**. The more or less that you have of **flexibility** and **determination** makes a lot of difference.

The other situational stuff, such as desires, goals and preferences, just pales in importance in most cases. Focus on **personality, flexibility, and determination** as we move on through some of the conflicts and decisions that need to be made. Add to these **humility** and a **sense of humor. Humility** allows you to not focus on your instantaneous analysis of the situation, but allows you to view and absorb the opinions of others. Your first thought may be perfectly right, but at least you allow for *critical thinking*. Think of yourself as an actor or actress in the *struggle of life* which repeats itself over and over again. Try to make it not too personal or too serious. We all have a tendency to jump to the *worst case scenario*. A **sense of humor** allows you to remove yourself from the scenario and look at your situation as if it were a play. It is not you or your other real-life characters... it is like watching a play or a movie. You'll be surprised if some acts of your play are not reminiscent of Jackie Gleason or other stars of comedy. I understand that your situation is serious, but you need to give yourself a break and relieve the intensity of the emotion. Your friends may be too closely allied to you to give you their frank opinion. So **personality, flexibility, determination** seasoned with **humility** and a **sense of humor** need to be your **tools.** Don't worry, this is not going to turn out to be a boring book filled with academic facts. This will be a practical handbook which you can use in daily life. If you simply keep those **5 factors** in mind you'll find that it helps a lot. But simply focus on **personality, flexibility** and **determination**.

XVI

# I

## EIGHT SELF-HELP TOOLS

Since this is a self-help book, we'll start with **you doing all the work**. I'm going to relax and avoid that terrible prison called work. Let's have some fun. We can approach a book like this in so many ways--each individual will hopefully glean something from these **tools** and put them into his own **toolbox**. Life is a pretty complicated experience filled with a lot of chaff which can often make it very difficult to navigate. It is filled with inconsistencies and contradictions. So let's begin.

### Be your own critic

Be your own self critic. We all tend to be self-centered, why not? I'm right... you're wrong! Am I really right? To what degree? Can I do anything to improve myself? Is there room for compromise or arbitration?

### What is important to you?

What are your hobbies and interests? What are your goals? What do you like? What do you dislike? Review these and see if they fall into the *important* or *unimportant* categories. If you see the need for any change, then look at your options.

### Increase your knowledge base

We've all come through an educational system whose informational base is very skewed. Be familiar with as many subjects as you can find....you will be surprised to find that you make many more friends. You're just a lot more interesting, and you can engage in some stimulating discussions with people who are interested in a variety of subjects. This can be done by anyone in less than a year, and without taking much time. It's really very simple – – if you read a beginner's book in 25 new fields you will enter the company of the top 5% of the most informed people in the world. Make that 50 books and you will be in the top 1%. It's pretty simple, and you can get most of the significant stuff by reading and skimming the content pretty fast. I don't care what the subject is – – just make it something new.

Think of a new sport, climate, animals, ceramics, art, trees, flowers, style, haute cuisine and couture, religions, history, lace, tapestry, literature, hobbies, architecture, woodworking and other trades, literature, cultures, nations, travel, famous books.... Pick any subject that you are unfamiliar with and you will be amazed how much you learn from just dabbling in the field. That is true of most things. The people who are highly educated in a field usually are dealing with the fundamentals, unless they are doing fundamental research. We walk by a lot of interesting stuff in our lives and don't have an inkling about the pleasure that we are missing. A good example of that is the oriental rug. There is a lot of history there and a lot to appreciate in many ways. So the next time that you walk by a store with an oriental rug in the window you'll be able to appreciate the quality, the designs, the quality of the colors and the people from whence all of that came.

You don't have to be very good to enjoy something. I have seen the staccato steps of the Irish, the powerful rhythm of el Greco with his one man hand-clapping accompaniment, the strong contrasting red and black colors of the Cossack dance troupe—the tall, elegant and powerful men...followed by the tall, striking an equally graceful and forceful women. The fine critic that I am, I was capable of reducing my evaluation of the American, French and Russian ballet companies to but a word...the Americans, competent, the French, graceful, the Russians, powerful! There are a lot of things to enjoy if you just give them a chance.

### Your role as an observer

Never say a word – – just observe what everyone else is doing. Why are they doing that? Is it productive? Does it work? Is it fun? Is it ridiculous? etc. Do you do any of these things?

Just spend a week doing this. If you find it productive, then continue for a bit longer. This is an adult project. Young people, and many adults, will be bored and just say, *"that's ridiculous!"*

### Be an actor/actress

This is your chance to be creative. This can be fun. We all come from parochial backgrounds and tend to move in pre-determined pathways. After all, we cannot know that which we do not know of. So think of yourself as an actor in different situations and see where that leads to. If you are in a difficult situation, this can be most useful, as you explore your options. And you thought you couldn't be creative! You'll probably have to hide what you're doing from others because they'll think that your a little queer.

## Stop the action

Don't do that. People tend to stop the process of growth once they are out of school and start working. Growth is a wonderful thing since it really is an enjoyable experience. You'll never get bored.

If you are a **doer** then continue to do many things. Continue to explore many fields of interests. If you find the experience to be pleasurable than continue; if not simply stop.

If you're a **thinker** you may be under the false impression that you are not a doer. You are naturally a productive person in so many ways, even if you are just sitting in a comfortable chair. There is so much to learn about musical history, the history of religions, etc. Then there is the history of literature and those wonderful novels. You can read about politicians, significant people and delve into the past and into the future. You can also read the eleven volumes of *The Story of Civilization* written by Will and Ariel Durant. Churchill's stuff can keep you busy for quite a while. You can always buy a lot of material from *The Great Courses*. You'll be surprised how much knowledge you can impart to others while having a normal conversation.

## Pleasure

**Creative Pleasure** is found in the person who is a participant in either a **doer** or **thinker** role. It is really based upon involvement and work. For example it takes 60 to 80,000 strokes in tennis to be competent at the game, and then to be really able to enjoy it.

**Passive Pleasure** is found in absorbing the work that others have done, such as listening to music, watching movies and television, watching sports. On a more active note there is the video game.

Are you in both categories? That's not a bad place.

## You're in the Bubble

Put yourself in a bubble and see what is controlling you and keeping you there. Is it your parents, your boss, your spouse, money, lack of education, taxes, friendship, location, obligation, standards, rules, etc.? Can you burst this bubble? How could you do that?

That's it. Read the books and play different roles. That's all there is to it. That's self-help! Close the book. Goodbye.

**What?! I have to continue writing more? More work? Life ain't fair!**

I may as well give you the tough stuff right at the very beginning. You do need to use *critical thinking*. You have to make sure that your thinking and conclusions are really solid. **Make sure that you're not jumping to conclusions**. It's very normal to jump to conclusions, so it's important to stop and make sure that you're really analyzing the facts. Slow down!

**You don't have to read this at this time**...you can come back to this once you've gone over the simple stuff. You may find that you don't really have to come back to this at all.

This following involves the concepts of fallacy, probability, validity, verifiability and falsifiability. If you start with a premise that is **false,** your conclusion is going to be wrong. A probability value is known as a **P value**. It is a measure of the statistical probability that your conclusion is either positive or negative. A **valid premise is supported by solid evidence leading to a solid conclusion**. The conclusion must be **verified** by your experience or observation (let's call that empirical data). That empirical data itself must be subject to the risk of being proven **false (falsifiability)**. So we'll make up formula. I'm sure that my use of the word formula is a misrepresentation of a concept which Spock would be heard to say, "it's illogical."

So **V (validity) = R (reliability) + F (falsifiability)**. For a premise to be valid it must fulfill both criteria: **V = R + F**. Science won't work if the equation is **V = R/F**. So let's outline some of the concepts having to do with **scientific validity**.

1 - A **false** premise leads to a wrong conclusion.
2 - **P value** is a measure of the statistical **probability** that your conclusion is either positive or negative.
3 - A **valid (validity)** premise is supported by solid evidence leading to a solid conclusion.

4

**4** - The conclusion must be **verified (verifiability)** by your experience or observation (let's call that empirical data).

**5** - That empirical data itself must be subject to the risk of being proven **false (falsifiability).** (don't worry about #5)

******

This is certainly a complicated way of looking at things. It's really quite simple. After you make an observation, you slow down your emotional response, activate your informational and logical systems, and come to some conclusion. It's usual and customary for us to look at issues in a very superficial fashion and move on. Beneath that skin that we observe, there are layers of reasons why we are exposed to that superficial view of the skin. Think of an issue as an onion. Peel one layer, and you find another layer, etc. We need to peel away the heuristic initial response(knee-jerk response) and look at the layer of logic that underlies it.

## WHAT ARE WE BATTLING... PERSONALITIES?

You may be getting the feeling that this book is just for eggheads or introspective people. But if you don't fit into those categories you'll be surprised to find some simple **tools** that will help you to deal with people problems. It's all common sense. I'm sure that you already are using some of these **tools**, so you can look at this as a refresher course. Were going to be following **rule #1** which must be consistent with **Occam's razor**...keep it as simple as you can. Simplify...don't get too complicated.

We do have to go over the fundamentals. This is primarily a book to help you navigate through issues which involve people. People are terribly complex creatures so that one formula does not fit all. It has always been my impression that it is best to let you, the reader, know as much is I do. This information should be useful to you as you are forced to encounter various personality types. We'll start by stating the obvious... **people are basically self-centered and selfish.**

Doctors talk in terms of understanding the difference between the disease and the symptoms. If an ooze is poisoning you, you can run away or go to the hospital. If you know that it is coming from an open pipe, you might consider capping it. Always remember that an expert's opinion must always be tempered by your common sense.

You'll probably conclude that this book is an exercise in naivety and a sneaky way of introducing **basic morality** to people who already are believers. The best interpersonal relationships are built upon **kindness** and **mutual self-respect**. We are constantly interacting with many personality types that are not interested in these two attributes. Many thrive on harming and abusing people. Our **tools** are designed to maximize your **positive impact** on others and to give you a good set of **self-defense tools** to minimize injury from people that it is in your best interest to avoid.

I'm not going to burden you with any academic material. We all know that every personality background involves the culture, whatever kind of parents are involved, the nature of the upbringing, the IQ, the education, people involvement and many other factors which can be quite random. We're not going to go into that...it's quicksand.

Keep in mind that we are highly **emotional** creatures. This leads us to make knee-jerk judgments based on all sorts of "pattern recognitions" and logical fallacies. Much has been written about this since Socratic times. You should remind yourself that it's important to **slow down, analyze** a situation using your logical gifts, and make an informed decision. That really doesn't happen all the time, but it increases the odds in your favor. History is filled with examples of logical decisions going nowhere. Things just happen. The economists use the term *ceteris paribus*, all things being equal, but that is rarely the case. Heisenberg said the same thing later on.

I'm going to ask you do shift from **participant** to **observer** and from **observer** to **participant** as we go along.

Calculus forces you to use **max/min**. You will have to keep that in mind as we go along. What are your *maximum and minimum* standards in evaluating your current situations and new goals? Are the standards realistic or just stuff that dreams are made of?

It's important to remember that the old saw, "if you're not going forward, you're falling behind," is really true. As we grow older, if we are not demonstrating any personal growth, then we are falling behind, we're losing friends, opportunities, etc. At least think about reading those books. I have a few to sell.

Rex Harrison said it very well, "Why can't they just be more like me?" We all grow up feeling as if people should feel and act as we do. You may argue with me about this, but I am right! But our expectations couldn't be further from the truth. People, their personalities, are so different. The psychiatric textbook tries to pigeonhole everyone into some sort of personality. That really isn't true. You'll find a smidgen of several personalities in any one dominant personality

I'm going to avoid discussing the criminal and juvenile delinquent types at this point and focus on the usual and customary people that we encounter. Some of the **best dressed personalities** can wreak a terrible hardship on people surrounding them. Hopefully you'll be able to avoid some of these people.

I'm going to introduce the concept of a **personality template**. This is where you align the various characteristics of each human personality and compare it to that of another person, such as a spouse.

There are so many that you can go on and on. You instantly understand why there are so many conflicts and divorces. I've put together a short list so that you get the general idea.

But first we must acknowledges there are differences between men and women. My daughter gave me this list for the women:

### Male & Female Personality Differences Template

| Male | Female |
|---|---|
| TV-football/sports in general | shopping |
| golfing | shoe shopping |
| fishing | crafts |
| boating | cooking |
| physically more powerful | manicures |
| short-term pleasures | cosmetics/perfumes |
| | hairstyling |
| | spas |
| | classical music |
| | opera |
| | long-term goals |
| | |

### Personality Template

| Male | Female |
|---|---|
| Age | Age |
| Significant family background | Significant family background |
| | |
| Superficial attributes | Superficial attributes |
| looks-handsome | looks-beautiful |

| | |
|---|---|
| attire-well groomed/sloppy | attire-well groomed/sloppy |
| casual ?/stylish | casual?/stylish |
| energetic | energetic |
| sociable | sociable |
| quiet | quiet |
| polite/offensive | polite/offensive |
| serious/sense of humor | serious/sense of humor |
| | |
| **Sexual interests** | **Sexual interests** |
| sexual frequency/interest | sexual frequency/interest |
| sexual capacity | sexual capacity |
| promiscuous | promiscuous |
| | |
| **Interests** | **Interests** |
| movies | movies |
| sports | sports |
| music | music |
| traveling | traveling |
| dining out | dining out |
| cultural events/museums | cultural events/museums |
| | |
| **Vacation preferences** | **Vacation preferences** |
| travel | travel |
| skiing | skiing |
| casino visiting | casino visiting |
| cruises | cruises |
| seashore activities | seashore activities |
| | |
| | |

| Hobbies | Hobbies |
|---|---|
| woodworking | crafts |
| car models | pets |
| | |
| **Pet peeves** | **Pet peeves** |
| washing dishes | washing dishes |
| being nagged | washing clothes |
| going to work | ironing |
| | procrastinating |
| | |
| **Strengths & weaknesses** | **Strengths & weaknesses** |
| basic intelligence-IQ | basic intelligence-IQ |
| educational level | educational level |
| common sense | common sense |
| neurotic? | neurotic |
| peculiarity? | peculiarity? |
| | |
| responsibility | responsibility |
| family | family |
| job-employment | job-employment |
| financial | financial |
| saves/spendthrift | saves/spendthrift |
| | |
| drug & alcohol addiction | drug & alcohol addiction |
| religious preference | religious preference |
| prejudices | prejudices |
| | |
| selfish/caring | selfish/caring |
| **Interactive skills** | **Interactive skills** |

11

| | |
|---|---|
| ability to compromise | ability to compromise |
| introspective/insightful | introspective/insightful |
| dogmatic | dogmatic |
| critical | critical |
| accepting | accepting |
| | |
| **Goals** | **Goals** |
| short and long-term | short and long-term |
| being successful in business | getting married |
| getting season football tickets | finishing school |
| finding the right girl | having children |
| | |

*I'm going to present you with an example. Look for the bold & italicized inserts in the column.*

## Personality Template

| Male | Female |
|---|---|
| **Age** | **Age** |
| **Significant family background** | **Significant family background** |
| | |
| **Superficial attributes** | **Superficial attributes** |
| looks-handsome | looks-beautiful |
| attire-well groomed/sloppy | attire-well groomed/sloppy |
| casual ?/stylish | casual?/stylish |
| *No energy* | *energetic* |
| *loner* | *sociable* |
| quiet | quiet |
| polite/offensive | polite/offensive |

| No sense of humor | Good sense of humor |
|---|---|
| **Sexual interests** | **Sexual interests** |
| sexual frequency/interest | sexual frequency/interest |
| sexual capacity | sexual capacity |
| Promiscuous *girlfriends* | *faithful* |
| | |
| **Interests** | **Interests** |
| movies | movies |
| *sports* | sports |
| music | *music* |
| traveling | traveling |
| *dining out spicy Mexican* | *dining out French & desserts* |
| cultural events/museums | cultural events/museums |
| | |
| **Vacation preferences** | **Vacation preferences** |
| travel | travel |
| skiing | *skiing* |
| *casino visiting* | casino visiting |
| cruises | cruises |
| seashore activities | seashore activities |
| | |
| **Hobbies** | **Hobbies** |
| crafts | woodworking |
| pets | car models |
| | |
| **Pet peeves** | **Pet peeves** |
| washing dishes | washing dishes |
| *being nagged* | washing clothes |

| | |
|---|---|
| going to work | ironing |
| | *procrastinating* |
| *Critical of wife* | *Critical of husband* |
| **Strengths & weaknesses** | **Strengths & weaknesses** |
| basic intelligence-IQ *average* | basic intelligence-IQ **high** |
| educational level | educational level |
| common sense | common sense |
| neurotic? | neurotic |
| peculiarity? | peculiarity? |
| | |
| *Responsibility gambles* | responsibility |
| family | family |
| job-employment | job-employment |
| *Financial low income* | *Financial saver -high income* |
| *spendthrift* | saves/spendthrift |
| *Selfish forgets the roses* | *Remembers his birthday* |
| drug & alcohol addiction | drug & alcohol addiction |
| *religious preference none* | *religious preference Catholic* |
| *Prejudices racial* | *Prejudices immigrants* |
| | |
| selfish/caring | selfish/caring |
| **Interactive skills** | **Interactive skills** |
| *ability to compromise never* | ability to compromise |
| introspective/insightful | *introspective/insightful* |
| dogmatic | dogmatic |
| *critical* | critical |
| accepting | accepting |
| | |
| | |

| Goals | Goals |
|---|---|
| short and long-term | short and long-term |
| being successful in business | getting married |
| getting season football tickets | finishing school |
| finding the right girl | *having children* |
| *Hates children* | |

So we see a married man who has *no energy, is a loner, has no sense of humor, has girlfriends, likes dining out and eating spicy Mexican food, he loves to gamble, he hates being nagged, he has average intelligence, he is a spendthrift, has a low income, is selfish and forgets the roses, has no religious preference, is racially prejudiced, never compromises and hates children.*

His wife is *energetic, sociable, has a good sense of humor, is faithful, loves music, likes to dine out in French restaurants and eat desserts, likes skiing, hates procrastinating, has a high IQ and a high income, is caring and remembers his birthday, has a Catholic preference, is introspective and insightful, is prejudiced towards immigrants and wants children.*

So you see that you can find out a lot about a relationship in just a few minutes. You'll find a set of **templates** at the end of the book that you can cut out and use at your pleasure.

UNVEILING PERSONALITY BEHAVIORS

You can add a lot more to that **personality template**. Even simplified, it is fairly complicated. In matching two templates we can find multiple areas that fit and other areas *which just do not fit.* Not surprising that there are so many divorces. It's time to look at a variety of personalities which have been simplified and would make the academic world cringe. Let's make a list of different people:

| | |
|---|---|
| **A Procrastinator** | **Responsible** |
| **Shy & Withdrawn** | **A Criminal** |
| **Paranoid** | **A Controller** |
| **Dependable** | **A Loner** |
| **Selfish** | **Unable to Take Care of** |
| **Alcoholic- Addict** | **Myself** |
| **A Worrier** | **An Obstructionist** |
| **An Actor** | **A User** |
| **A Leader** | **Neurotic & Self-centered** |
| **A Perfectionist** | **Serious & Unemotional** |

**A Procrastinator** is possibly the most cunning and insidious type. You then say, "he's always late." He's always creating anxiety around him. If he simply fails to tell you about vacation time, his schedule, his expectation of meeting his every desire... then you are in a real pickle. You even sound rather silly if you tell your friends about this. The behavior may have started as part of a personality quirk, but it is now done reflexively and deliberately... since the nature of the game is to enjoy irritating people... *perverse enjoyment.*
     **Strategy**: Never show any irritation. Simply say, " I wish I would have known." "What would you like to do?"..... "It's too bad that you missed out on something." It's a matter of putting the responsibility on him without saying that it is what you're doing. Humor... humor... difficult to do.

     **Shy & Withdrawn** may have many good qualities but fears rejection. Family encouragement fails to do very much. Tends to be very helpful if given a specific task.
     **Strategy**: Personal self-improvement is the key. Encourage development of hobbies and interests. Further education and obtaining a good job helps to bump into someone who can relate to

the qualities in the individual.

**Paranoid** can be graded on a bell shaped curve. Sometimes it shows itself as a streak of jealousy, other times as too much belief in conspiracy theories. This person tends to react negatively to anything that you do.

**Strategy**: Avoid this person. He'll be accusing you. You can't possibly explain the situation to his liking. If you refuse to discuss the situation, he will only get more paranoid. Keep your discussions at an informational level without any commentary or value judgments. Simply ask him what he thinks about the issue. He will feel much better venting his irritation and anger and suspicions.

**Dependable**: This sounds like the perfect person. It certainly is a virtue. He may be so dependable because he is in a rut. If he is dependable and responsible and takes initiative, then it is a wonderful mixture.

**Strategy**: Be appreciative. Be the initiator if that is needed. Share your interests and goals with him.

**Selfish**: this is a difficult person to live with since he does not care about the feelings of others.

**Strategy**: Do not expect him to do anything for you. Be pleasantly surprised if that occasionally happens. Make sure that you are in control of anything that is essential to you and your children. Be in control of some of the finances. That's the way it has to be.

**Alcoholic-Addict**: .This may be a chronic problem or only intermittent. His behaviors may be erratic, but he may be a good person who does his best otherwise.

**Strategy**: Get rid of this guy if he is irresponsible, unable to support you or is just plain cruel. You really can't afford to destroy your life and the life of your children around a fellow like that. You'll have to weigh the pros and cons if you're living with someone like this. As you can see I use the **him** and not the **her** but all this stuff applies equally to either.

**A Worrier**: This person is obviously quite insecure. He often can't differentiate between important and unimportant things.

**Strategy**: You can't stop him from worrying. Just repeatedly point out the reality of the situation and say, "it will be okay." Always be reassuring. It gets very tiresome, so make sure that you are involved in something that you really enjoy.

18

**An Actor**: This is okay if this does not cause problems. This may be his way of feeling important or he may simply be having good fun. If the acting hides some pretty bad behaviors, then you are in trouble. The private person could be pretty bad.

**Strategy**: Be supportive if his private life is good. If his secret *persona* gives you a lot of grief, then you have to deal with it in a straightforward fashion.

**A Leader**: This sounds like a good person to be close to. He may carry you into a wonderful world. But if that leadership is only ego driven, you may be along for a bumpy ride.

**Strategy**: Some leaders forget that they have responsibilities to the people that are really close to them. You can only explain what the consequences of his actions are for you, and see what happens.

**A Perfectionist**: Virtue or vice? He can drive you crazy if he nitpicks everything. Keeping the house spiffy may be really cool. Anything in excess is always an irritant, but you need to accept it if you understand the motivation to be good. It's not unusual for someone to dress perfectly only to find that his home is a mess.

**Strategy**: Very little can be done if a person is driven to be a perfectionist. You really have to learn to accept and overlook it. Figure out a way of getting around it if it is an area essential to your functioning.

**Responsible**: This sounds a lot like **dependable**. There is an essential difference. This man thinks ahead and plans to make positive things happen. He handles problems as they come along.

**Strategy**: You can openly discuss your side of any issue and work out reasonable options.

**A Criminal**: There is a range of behaviors here. Best to be far away from this person if cruelty and evil are part of the package.

**Strategy**: Stay away from the cruelty and evil package. Some are good to their families. The issue comes down to stability, money, effect on children, etc. You have to use your common sense in dealing with these issues.

**A Controller**: This guy can drive you crazy. You have to get permission to do anything and have to explain any of your actions. He really is a neurotic *stiff* which an observer would find to be pretty funny, not so if you are part of the action.

**Strategy**: Walk away if you can't put up with this. Otherwise you have to see the humor in this. Then you just play along with all of this without getting upset. Tell your children that that he really cares, and that he does not realize that it bothers them. Meanwhile live your secret and very private world in whatever way it works.

**A Loner**: This person either fears people or has no use for them. He may be a very intelligent and talented person.
**Strategy**: Give him his space. He's not going to change. You may stumble upon his areas of interests and find that you get along pretty well. Don't be pushy, he'll only resent it.

**Unable to Take Care of Myself**: This person may be a hypochondriac and/or simply unable to take any responsibility.
**Strategy**: You really can't do anything about a situation like this. Avoid, avoid... if you can. Otherwise your simply into damage control. Be as supportive as you can, but do what you must do... have a life apart from the prison that you find yourself in.

**An Obstructionist**: This person may suffer from *yeah..but..itis*. It's fairly common with teenagers but it gets really old when you find it in adults. This person always comes up with an objection and the negative side of any issue. He can stop you from having any fun. He can always find an objection to going to a movie, going on vacation or having friends over.
**Strategy**: Just plan and do things without any discussion. Most likely he'll just go along, but with his usual expression of anger. Just find the humor in this and have a good time. If he won't go along, then just plan that your adventures will be without him.

**A User**: This chap is into the *gimme mode* and will just take as much as he can. He'll use you in any way that you allow him to use you. He'll also take your things and not return them. He was probably pretty spoiled as a kid, and you're not going to teach him how to grow up and be a big boy.
**Strategy**: It's simple, measure your donations to this *poor boy* as a charitable act. Give only what you can afford spiritually so that you can live a normal, healthy life. He won't be happy about that, but alas!... there is suffering everywhere.

**Neurotic & Self-centered**: This guy is a mess. He may find some pleasure in an activity, but otherwise his entire world is one of walling off the invaders. Things out of place, things that never happen, the unexpected happening... these cause him such inconveniences and bother him so. Humorous and pathetic. Everyone is to blame for these imaginary assaults on his fortifications.

**Strategy**: This guy will drive you crazy if you let him. He is convinced that he is in the right... all the time. You are part of this play that creates so much pain for him on a daily basis. Don't listen to it. Make your plans as if he didn't exist. Don't get angry... it only gives him the opportunity to blame you and to give you some crazy excuse... *meshugana.* You must **be in control** when you're involved with an out of control individual.

**Serious & Unemotional**: He may have some very good character traits, but he really does not have time to have real fun.

**Strategy**: If he is a very dependable individual, then it's just a matter of accepting his nature. Try to explain to him why you are doing things or have certain interests. He probably will appreciate that.

Are you getting tired of this? I assume that you can think of some individuals who exhibit these types of behaviors, many with an admixture. There really is no pure culture. That's why the gourmet offerings of the expert have to have some seasoning added to them. **Why don't you see if you can make up a few personality profiles on your own...after observing a few people around you.**

******

**What are his characteristics?** Put something in here that are the dominant features.

**Strategy:** What are the various ways that you could reasonably interact with a person like that?

**Are you starting to get the hang of this?**

## IV

## IN CONTROL OF DIALOGUE

The importance of **being in control** can't be overemphasized. **Never lose control** even when your getting hot under the collar, even when you're losing. This chapter will help you to **control the dialogue**. You might be able to visualize this as if you were a **prize fighter**... feeling out your opponent.

****** 

**Begin by being in control of yourself with
HUMILITY & HUMOR
Avoid Arrogance**

******

**Strategy:** Always make your friend or foe feel important and in control.

**Tactic**: Let your friend or foe give his opinion right up front. Find out where he is coming from and if he has already made a decision. It saves a lot of time. You are already judging his **flexibility** and **determination**.

Always ask for **clarification** of the issues, and politely ask for his **reasons**.

Ask him if he has looked at **other possibilities**.

**Never reveal your goal or intention.**

Offer **other reasonable options** which would be secondary options. Don't indicate that you have any preferences.

Gradually reveal that you have found a few flaws in the options.

Begin to offer **suggestions**. Gradually give him a list of **options that you could agree with.** Consider that you are always in a **max/min** situation. Remember, you are not a patsy.

With **humility** and **humor** you will be standing **firm.** Think of yourself as a fighter... you **don't have to win**... you **can be satisfied with a draw.** You just don't want to be a victim of a **KO.**

\*\*\*\*\*\*

**For those of you who enjoy looking at a formula:**

**SELF CONTROL = humility + humor + firmness/arrogance**
**SELF CONTROL = H+H+F/A**

\*\*\*\*\*\*

Start by analyzing any issue with *critical thinking:*

**1-Define the issue.** The cause, the **why?,** may or may not have any relevance.
**2-Your initial wishes** – possible expectations, goals and solutions.
**3-Disable emotions. Use logic.**
**4-Review all the facts.**
**5-List of options.**
        **a-What's best for *me* in the short term?**
        **b-What's best for *me* in the long term?**
        **c-What's best for *others* in the short term?**
        **d-What's best for *others* in the long-term?**

So you can see that *you're in control of yourself*, regardless of the quality or the wisdom of your decision.

\*\*\*\*\*\*

So we need to move into being *in control of the dialogue*, remembering that we are dealing with **a personality,** his **flexibility**, his **determination** coupled with **humility & humor.** Keep **P+F+D** in mind. **PDF** is easier for the Internet user.

\*\*\*\*\*\*

Prepare yourself for the dialogue by analyzing any issue with *critical thinking:*

1-**Define the issue.** The cause, the **why?**, may or may not have any relevance.
2-**Your initial wishes** – possible expectations, goals and solutions.
3-**Disable emotions. Use logic.**
4-**Review all the facts.**
5-**List of options.**
      a-**What's best for *me* in the short term?**
      b-**What's best for *me* in the long term?**
      c-**What's best for *others* in the short term?**
      d-**What's best for *others* in the long-term?**

******

**Prepared, it's time *to confront*:**

**Personality Type
Flexibility
Determination**


**Let's get back to being *in control of the dialogue*:**

**Be in charge
Slowdown
No rapid responses
The background is one of Humility and Humor
Be Firm not Arrogant**

******

**Strategy:** Always make your friend or foe feel important and in control.

**Tactic**: Let your friend or foe give his opinion right up front . Find out where he is coming from and if he has already has made a decision. It saves a lot of time. You are already judging his **flexibility** and **determination**.

Always ask for **clarification** of the issues, and politely ask for his **reasons**.

Ask him if he has looked at **other possibilities**.

**Never reveal your goal or intention.**

Offer **other reasonable options** which would be secondary options. Don't indicate that you have any preferences.

Gradually reveal that you have found a few flaws in the options.

Begin to offer **suggestions**. Gradually give him a list of **options that you could agree with.** Consider that you are always in a **max/min** situation. Remember, you are not a patsy. With **humility** and **humor** you will be standing **firm.** Think of yourself as a fighter... you **don't have to win**... you **can be satisfied with a draw.** You just don't want to be a victim of a **KO.**

**Think of your interactions in this manner:**

**1-Ask his opinion. Don't tell him what you want.**
**2-Await his response**
**3-Raise your questions and options**
**4-Await his answer**

**Continue in this fashion**

Approaching an **issue** in this way will help you to clarify how he feels about an issue, whether he has thought about it, how flexible he is and how to best approach the situation. You may change your mind as you go along. See if you have enough flexibility in yourself to move in a different direction. Anyway, you'll be on a lot firmer footing for the next bout....**if you're a good and fair fighter.**

## V

## EDUCATION

To maximize our effectiveness in life, we must use our **tools**, which are enhanced by our education, our experience and our overall knowledge. You know much of what's in this chapter, but it brings our ideas to life if we are forced to review such things.

There's much that's wrong with our current educational model. We learn things in chunks of disparate topics. We do not integrate what we have learned. We memorize a lot. We have cut out vocational schools. We are told that all children have to go to college, and that they then have to go to graduate school to specialize. When hired the employer has to give them one to two years of on-the-job training for them to be of any use. I've written about the need to change our educational system so that it is upside down in my book *Requiem for American Critical Thinking & Democracy,* but that is a whole different topic.

You can be of great help to your children if you can teach them a lot of stuff as they are growing up. Children are naturally very inquisitive and you will find it hard to answer all of the questions. But you can give them some good **tools**. The basics of cooking are often omitted; the boys should be taught. Teach them how to use a needle and thread, a hammer, nails, a screwdriver, the Allen and Phillip's head screws, the wrenches, the fuses, the electric box breakers, where the handles are to turn off the water when the apartment is being flooded, the basics of electricity, plumbing, carpentry and what is necessary and best for the dogs and cats. There's a lot more but you get the general idea. Both the girls and boys will thank you for your efforts. You see how frustrated people get when they don't know the basics in an emergency.

Adults tend to do things without sharing the how and why with their kids. Knowing something about Social Security, credit cards, banking and all those licenses is a great help. Kids can get a great education just by being around parents who answer questions and share their knowledge with them.

Children grow up with the computer and learn that as naturally as they do their native language. That's not necessarily good since all that focus on video games and the Internet ends up significantly decreasing their social skill building set. There are always trade-offs and that's why there are parents hired to take care of the kids.

Many adults tend to stop their learning process once they finish school and get a job. You can have a much fuller life if you keep on asking **why?, why?, why?**...just like the kids. There is a ton of interesting material that we can continue to grow into. **Why stop?**

**Just a thought**....if your friend or significant other is really into something, why not learn something about it? It might just add some vibrancy to your relationship. Most people find most things to be interesting... once they learn something about the basics.

**How's that for a short chapter!** "A man's got to know his limits."

## VI

## DATING

The **dating tool** which I shall now offer will probably get this reaction, "**it just doesn't make any sense.**" The dating game isn't a game...it's deadly serious. Everyone wants to be popular and have friends. So you do everything you can to be liked, except for those extremely popular kids who can be can be quite cruel towards others. Adolescents should avoid those people like the plague, rather than doing anything to be liked by them. They are only forming a bad character trait by becoming **people-pleasers**.

The **dating game** should be understood to have two parts to it. The **first part** is learning to have fun with your friends and the new dating partner. You should learn everything that you can about him or her, and don't be shy about asking **why?** You learn a great deal about people in that way, and you certainly should not be offensive in your manner. It's all about learning about people while you're having fun.

Kids don't like to listen to their parents... but they've heard it loud and clear It's best not to have **a steady** throughout high school because you're not exploring the range of behaviors and personality types that are out there. Kids have trouble giving up something that is safe. We can all understand that.

Then comes **part two**. Once you have had a lot of fun, be sure not to be a **people-pleaser**. This is the time to explore the long-term potential of your relationship. Get to know your boyfriend or girlfriend better... what does he think about his parents?, what does he think that he could do to improve himself?, why does he hang around with his friends?, is he doing the best that he could at school or at work?, where is he headed?, what are his long-term goals? You certainly can pry and challenge in a most congenial way.

The **dating game** is fun. You'd have to be crazy to be talking about work and responsibility. The long haul... the long term relationship... is all about that... work, paying the bills, cooking, cleaning, fixing the car, taking care of the kids and doing a whole lot of things that can't be classified as fun.

So the **dating tool** is to **turn the fun switch off** after you've had a whole lot of fun, and **ask probing questions** to find out what mettle your date is made of. **Mettle** is the keyword here, defined as, "a person's ability to cope well with difficulties or to face a demanding situation in a spirited and resilient way." I would hate to be measured by that parameter. Most relationships would probably be terminal using that criteria. So you see that you can only listen to me up to a point. Maybe this is time to abandon ship.

This is probably a good time to look at the short form of the **Personality Template.**

## Short Personality Template

| Male | Female |
|---|---|
| **Age** | **Age** |
| **Superficial attributes** | **Superficial attributes** |
| looks and personality | looks and personality |
| | |
| **Sexual interests** | **Sexual interests** |
| Now or later? | Now or later? |
| **Interests** | **Interests** |
| activities/hobbies | activities/hobbies |
| | |
| **Pet peeves** | **Pet peeves** |
| | |
| **Strengths & weaknesses** | **Strengths & weaknesses** |
| | |
| **Level of responsibility** | **Level of responsibility** |
| | |
| **Interactive skills** | **Interactive skills** |
| compromise/insightful | compromise/insightful |
| | |

| Marriage | Marriage |
|---|---|
| time together | time together |
| | |
| **Financial security** | **Financial security** |
| | |
| **Children** | **Children** |
| Do you want children? | Do you want children? |
| | |
| **Goals** | **Goals** |
| short and long-term | short and long-term |
| | |

You know how to do this. Plug-in the appropriate characteristics under these headings and get a feeling for the short and long-term potentials in your **dating game**.

## VII

## HUSBAND – WIFE - SIGNIFICANT OTHER NEGOTIATIONS

     This is really an important chapter since 50% of marriages **end** in **divorce**. It would really be nice if these tools ended up in salvaging a troubled relationship, especially if **children** are involved. They are the ones who truly suffer. So let's get on with it. What **tools** do we have?

### PFD
### Personality-Flexibility-Determination

### HHF/A
### Humility-Humor-Flexibility/Arrogance

### Kindness-Mutual Self Respect

     Let's take a look at the template that we'll be using in this exercise. You may want to review the **Personality Template** which you can find at the end of the book. After all you might as well review the type of person that you chose to be with.

### HUSBAND-WIFE-SIGNIFICANT OTHER TEMPLATE

| Male/Female | Female/Male |
|---|---|
| **Husband** | **Wife** |
| **Age** | **Age** |
| caring/distant | caring/distant |
| individual time | individual time |
| | |
| time together | time together |
| | |
| communicative | communicative |

| | |
|---|---|
| open and honest/sharing | open and honest/sharing |
| movie/dining out together | movie/dining out together |
| | |
| **Sexual behaviors** | **Sexual behaviors** |
| | |
| **Financial security** | **Financial security** |
| job stability | job stability |
| good income | good income |
| | |
| **Children** | **Children** |
| wanted? | wanted? |
| cares for/dislikes? | cares for/dislikes? |
| family eats together | family eats together |
| | |
| spends time with them | spends time with them |
| answers their questions | answers their questions |
| takes them places | takes them places |
| takes them on vacations | takes them on vacations |
| goes to school programs | goes to school programs |
| limits TV/video time | limits TV/video time |
| | |
| **Goals** | **Goals** |
| short and long-term | short and long-term |
| building a pension | buying a house |
| saving money | getting the kids into college |
| | |

**So you now have a list of
good and bad
likes and dislikes**

**It's time to *choose The Issue***

Limit it to one issue at a time. Give it time to cool and settle in. Come back to it when you both have time to cool off.

Remember that a good relationship is built upon **Humility & Humor** and the important ingredients are **Kindness & Mutual Self Respect.** Remember to say thank-you a lot and to give some compliments whenever you can. Don't be angry, irritable or confrontational, unless there is no other way. Be cool. Remember... **you don't have to win**... you **can be satisfied with a draw.** You just don't want to be a victim of a **KO.**

So what are the **issues?**

| Husband | Wife |
|---|---|
| time together- more time with my friends | time together-seems to be avoiding me |

| Sexual behaviors | Sexual behaviors |
|---|---|
| She seems colder | We haven't had sex in weeks |

It would appear that something is going on. Time for some verbal interaction. Review the beginning of the dialogue chapter and begin.

**Think of your interactions in this manner:**

**Bring up *the issue***

**1-Ask his opinion. Don't tell him what you want.
2-Await his response
3-Raise your questions and options
4-Await his answer**

**Continue in this fashion**

So what if it all falls apart and you end up in a **divorce**? You have a 50-50 chance of having this happen to you. Remember that your partner may turn out to be a rather vindictive and vicious individual... especially if he or she feels double-crossed. And many people turn out to be rather nasty when the issue of money is raised. Lawyers always want the money up front for good reason. These are the issues that you have to think about:

      **1- alimony and child support**
      **2- child custody**
      **3- visitation time**
      **4- one parent teaching the child to hate the other parent**
      **5- expectation of your ex adhering to the contract**
      **6- dirty linen exposed**
      **7- impact on the children**

Many children do not deal with divorce is very well. There are many reasons for that. I always remember talking to a lady who was working on her fifth marriage which had difficulties. I asked, "why aren't you getting a divorce if you're finding the going so tough?" The answer was pretty prompt, "I finally learned that there are difficulties in all marriages." That little piece of dialogue is true... you can decide if it contains silliness or wisdom or both. So before you decide on that divorce, you might just look at that **personality template** again.

# VIII

## LEARNING ABOUT CHILDREN
### or
### HOW DID I GET MYSELF INTO THIS MESS?

I'm sure you wondered why you ran into a blank page. That's probably where this chapter should've ended since the rearing of children is such a mystery to us. Many experts feel that they have a good handle on this. But any on-the-job parent will tell you that what works on one day, just doesn't work on the next day. You might as well join the dart throwing group at the Wall Street Journal or join the crowd at the roulette wheel in Las Vegas.

My dad used to tell us about a family known as the 6 Gun..s. Five of them were lawyers who were kept busy trying to keep the 6th Gun..out of jail. The **tools of the trade** are **humility, humor, a good set of rules, fairness, firmness & consequences.** You can now go to the next chapter. A parent has to be both a **teacher** and a **disciplinarian**.

Children come in all varieties and there appears to be ample evidence that their characters are formed somewhere between ages 2 to 5. I guess one would have to conclude that it is the job of the parent to do something about this... if the gene can be modified , if possible.

We know that children are born with natural assets in terms of size, shape, length, energy, intelligence....that sort of thing. They are also very naturally inquisitive creatures. They enter a world in which they have no control....culture and parents. The reader of this book has little control over the culture. The parent is essentially going to be the only teacher for the next five years and brings knowledge and effort into the equation of growth and development. The more the parent knows, the more the child can learn if the parent is willing to answer those multiple questions.

The parent sets the **rules** and implements the **discipline**. Civility and discipline standards have been lowered in the culture and at home in the past few generations. The American standard of homework is two hours per week, the kids never fail and the problems in school are blamed on the teachers. The parents haven't been doing their job at home. Many of those hyperkinetic kids have never been exposed to discipline at home. What's a teacher to do?

If you are an interested parent you probably have been reading books on all of this stuff, so I won't bore you. Remember to limit the TV time. Teach the ABCs, letters, words, how to spell their names and to start reading some simple books. It's time-consuming, **it's tiring, it's frustrating and it drives any normal parent crazy.** The **tools of the**

**trade** are **humility, humor, a good set of rules, fairness, firmness & consequences.**

Exposing children to the zoo, the aquarium, the children's museum, cultural events, parades and a ton of those nature and history DVDs is both fun and good schooling.

The parent's expectations have to be **age-appropriate.** *You can't expect the kid to act like a grown up.* You have to be able to remove yourself from the **participant in deadly combat** to the role of **the teacher** who is **kind** and has a **sense of humor.**

Parents also come in all varieties so they may need some upgrading in certain areas. I know that all the stories that I was exposed to can't even be found in the library anymore. Dick and Jane books are part of prehistory.

Put together an outline of what you can offer your kids. You can get a lot of information by simply talking to a friendly teacher before your kids ever go to school. The librarian in the children's section is a great source of what your children need to get involved in.

The kids will grumble about all the schooling that you're going to force them to be involved in it home. But since you love them and are kind to them, they'll get over it and actually enjoy most of it.

Children don't have to be taught anything about the computers and the video games. They are at an age where they learn that as easily as their native language. It's a cop-out to keep them on the TV and playing their computer games so that you can just get away from it all. However, you can choose some pretty good stuff such as ABC mouse.com.

## IX

## THE QUICKSAND OF ADOLESCENCE

Enter the **Age of Exploration**. The teenagers are experiencing the changes occurring to their bodies, and they spend a great deal of time trying to make themselves look handsome and beautiful. The need to be liked and popular is exceptionally strong. Bonding with a few friends and with a boyfriend or girlfriend seems to overwhelm the entire stage. But let us not tarry, this is a book about having the **tools** needed to cope with this critical period.

How do you expect the adolescents to relate to the parents? Some want to be very close to their parents and want the parents to teach them things. The others tend to resist time with the parents and being taught anything. The parents may, likewise, want or not want to spend time and teach their children.

Many parents are either controllers or simply want to do the best that they can for their children. The teenager will resent your being too pushy. Remember that the economic *law of diminishing returns* applies. A 90% effort brings a 96% rate of return. A 99% effort brings a 96.5% rate of return. It's not your fault, that's the way it is.

It's good to keep in mind that you represent the **Age of Reason.** The teenager is moving in that direction, but don't treat him as if he has to be there already. This is just another developmental stage. Remember that you have to respect **age appropriate behaviors** and not expect him to act like **adults are expected to act**. Don't get angry... even if it's a normal and expected response. **Always be in control**. That's a repetitive theme.

**Let's look at your toolbox:**

**1- kindness**
**2- mutual self-respect-but you are the boss**
**3- rule maker**
**4- fairness**
**5- consistency**
**6- negotiator-open to options**

******

## The environment

1- parent is always available for discussion
2- tradition of a sit-down family dinner
3- family members each take a turn at coming up with a topic which interests him or her and reporting on it. Can be a daily or a weekly project. Encourage discussions about daily events
4- know and invite the friends of your adolescent to dinner
5- meet the teachers and participate in school projects
6- encourage activities such as the taking of music lessons
7- make everyone feel special. Have parties, especially birthday parties
8- "what would you like to do?"
9- schoolwork takes precedence over fun. That is the **job of the adolescent** at this stage. Limit the phone, TV and video time

This is just a suggested routine in a positive environment. You know what is best in your own environment, but there has to be a **glue to the family** since there is a strong tendency to drift apart and "do your own thing." I know that you're getting bored.... you know all this stuff... but do you actually do it? It's actually fairly tough to do since it takes adult discipline and determination... parents have their own needs.

## Rules of the road

1- you set the rules-explain why-consequences
2- anticipate issues and problems and discuss them with your adolescent.... sex-drugs-stealing, etc.
3- spend private time with the adolescent
4- know what the activities are for the forthcoming week
5- encourage any positive interest or activity
6- give praise and advice
7- be open to negotiate...review options
8- feel free to confront and explain that an adolescent has a limited right to privacy when appropriate. The adolescent has a right to complain

A parent can take the attitude that adolescence is simply a **time of survival** and just get the kid through until he's 18 and then he can find himself a job. An alternative is to see yourself as a teacher exposing your children to as many topics and adventures which surround them in the world. Essentials like cooking should probably be taught to both boys and girls and given an international flavor...just to whet their appetite...so to speak. The more the kids know about things, the more they will really enjoy life and be enjoyable to others. It's a bit of a fight to go against the adolescent's natural proclivities of dating, doing the music thing and eating plenty of junk food. Do the **max/min** thing and see what your goals are for your children. See what can be accomplished. But above all do not belabor what you wish them to do..it only forces them to dig in their heels and prevents your wishes from happening. That's where the **law of diminishing returns** is proven in a rather scientific way.

I promised you short chapters and oversimplification. I guess I'm on track.

# X

## WORK-YOU & THE BOSS

This is **not** a chapter on how to get a job. There are plenty of books on that. There are, of course, several general principles. You always come for your interview appropriately dressed... no high heels if you're applying for a roofer's job. You should be pleasant and well mannered. Answer the questions briefly, demonstrating that you understand the question and your answers are based upon some knowledge and experience. If you are asked if you have any questions, answer with questions that are pertinent to the job... not about the benefits. You certainly should come prepared with some information about the company...large or small, self-employed, etc. That's all I'm going to say about it...and I'm sure that the experts will immediately disagree with what I have just written. But I have some umbrage... I'm no expert.

It matters what your short-term and long-term goals are, whether you are a part-time or a full-time employee, whether you are still in school, married, have children, etc.

To be a good employee you need to be **prompt, loyal, flexible, have a good attitude and show some initiative. You have to be able to get along with your fellow employees.** These are your **tools**. Given that...remember that the boss *is the boss*. You may think that he's stupid, but shut up and don't talk like that with your fellow employees. Once you are an established employee you can find ways of offering your ideas and improvements or modifications as you go along and are respected. Don't get the impression that you are a valued employee as you step into your new job... unless you are being hired for your expertise and for a specific purpose.

\*\*\*\*\*\*

It's time to look at another **personality template**... This one is about the boss:

## Boss – Manager Template

| Boss | You |
|---|---|
| **Male or female** | is that a problem? |
| **Age** | **Age** |
| **Type of industry** | |
| **Superficial attributes** | |
| grooming-attire | do you like him? |
| isolates | |
| works with employees | |
| irritable and critical | |
| well respected | |
| hated | |
| productivity at any cost | |
| | |
| **Personal interests** | |
| keeps to himself | |
| well-known to employees | |
| | |
| **Strengths & weaknesses** | |
| smart | |
| common sense | |
| peculiarities? | |
| predictable | |
| can hold a grudge | |
| alcoholic? | |
| open to new ideas | |
| **Goals** | |
| maximize profits | can you work with him? |
| employee participation in benefits | |

If the pay is right, and you can deal with that **boss-manager template**, then it seems to be an adequate fit...for the short term at least.

If you have any issues, recommendations or thoughts that you would like to have him consider, then you can move towards incorporating some of the stuff from the **dialogue chapter.**

> **Strategy:** Always make your boss feel important and in control...start with something like this, "I like working here..."

> **Raise your issue**: Raise your issue in the form of a question, asking him for his opinion about it.

> **Tactic**: Let your boss give his opinion right up front. Find out where he's coming from and if he has already made a decision. It saves a lot of time. You are already judging his **flexibility** and **determination**.

> Always ask for **clarification** of the issues, and politely ask for his **reasons**.

> Ask him if he has looked at **other possibilities**.

> **Don't reveal your final intention.**

> Offer **other reasonable options** which would be secondary options. Don't indicate that you have any preferences.

> Gradually reveal that you have found a few flaws in the options.

Begin to offer **suggestions**. Gradually give him a list of **options that you could agree with.** Consider that you are always in a **max/min** situation. With **humility** and **humor** you will be standing **firm.** Think of yourself as a fighter... you **don't have to win**... you **can be satisfied with a draw**. You just don't want to be a victim of a **KO.** If he's not inclined to agree with your analysis, then walk away with **humility & humor**..."thanks for the time, I just thought I'd run that by you."

**Think of your interactions in this manner:**

**Bring up the issue**

**1-Ask his opinion. Don't tell him what your goal is.**
**2-Await his response**
**3-Raise your questions and options**
**4- Await his answer**

**Continue in this fashion**

# XI

## TOOLS FOR THE FUTURE

I promised you a short book... so the rest is is just the highlights. Think of reevaluating your situation every 5 to 10 years and resetting goals.

### YOUNG ADULTHOOD

1- developing personal skills
2- finding employment and continue improving skills
3- working on relationships and possible marriage
4- raising children-buying life insurance
5- earning possessions such as car and home
6- becoming financially responsible
7- savings and pension for the future

### MIDDLE AGE

1- pursuing job security
2- stabilized marriage or divorce
3- putting kids through school
4- enjoying the fruits of your labor
5- starting to focus on retirement needs

### OLD AGE-RETIREMENT

1- financial independence
2- living separate from the family
3- living with the kids
4- decrease in physical and mental facilities-strokes, arthritis, diabetes, heart attacks etc.
5- time on your hands-travel, hobbies etc.

It's hard to do, but you should be doing some planning for the future when you are still very young. Money compounds very nicely, so it is very wise to put little chunks in on a regular basis – – toward your retirement. Do you best – – the future is an unknown. Go bravely into that unknown.

# EPILOGUE

You have to admit that this **bag of tools** is considerably lighter than the toolbox carried by the average tradesman. You can refer to the following list of **templates** as needed.

**Male & Female Personality Differences Template**
**Page 9**

**Personality Template**
**Page 9**

**Short Personality Template**
**Page 30**

**Husband-Wife-Significant Other Template**
**Page 33**

**Boss-Manager Template**
**Page 46**

**Two sets of templates follow. You can use a sharp blade and cut out one set. Photocopy that set so that you can use them as** *useful tools* **in everyday life. You might even make a party game out of them.**

## Male & Female Personality Differences Template

| Male | Female |
|---|---|
| TV-football/sports in general | shopping |
| golfing | shoe shopping |
| fishing | crafts |
| boating | cooking |
| physically more powerful | manicures |
| short-term pleasures | cosmetics/perfumes |
| | hairstyling |
| | spas |
| | classical music |
| | opera |
| | long-term goals |
| | |

# Personality Template

| Male | Female |
|---|---|
| **Age** | **Age** |
| **Significant family background** | **Significant family background** |
| | |
| **Superficial attributes** | **Superficial attributes** |
| looks-handsome | looks-beautiful |
| attire-well groomed/sloppy | attire-well groomed/sloppy |
| casual ?/stylish | casual?/stylish |
| energetic | energetic |
| sociable | sociable |
| quiet | quiet |
| polite/offensive | polite/offensive |
| serious/sense of humor | serious/sense of humor |
| | |
| **Sexual interests** | **Sexual interests** |
| sexual frequency/interest | sexual frequency/interest |
| sexual capacity | sexual capacity |
| promiscuous | promiscuous |
| | |
| **Interests** | **Interests** |
| movies | movies |
| sports | sports |
| music | music |
| traveling | traveling |
| dining out | dining out |
| cultural events/museums | cultural events/museums |
| | |

| Vacation preferences | Vacation preferences |
| --- | --- |
| travel | travel |
| skiing | skiing |
| casino visiting | casino visiting |
| cruises | cruises |
| seashore activities | seashore activities |
| | |
| **Hobbies** | **Hobbies** |
| crafts | woodworking |
| pets | car models |
| | |
| **Pet peeves** | **Pet peeves** |
| washing dishes | washing dishes |
| being nagged | washing clothes |
| going to work | ironing |
| | procrastinating |
| | |
| **Strengths & weaknesses** | **Strengths & weaknesses** |
| basic intelligence-IQ | basic intelligence-IQ |
| educational level | educational level |
| common sense | common sense |
| neurotic? | neurotic |
| peculiarity? | peculiarity? |
| | |
| responsibility | responsibility |
| family | family |
| job-employment | job-employment |
| financial | financial |
| saves/spendthrift | saves/spendthrift |

| | |
|---|---|
| drug & alcohol addiction | drug & alcohol addiction |
| religious preference | religious preference |
| prejudices | prejudices |
| | |
| selfish/caring | selfish/caring |
| **Interactive skills** | **Interactive skills** |
| ability to compromise | ability to compromise |
| introspective/insightful | introspective/insightful |
| dogmatic | dogmatic |
| critical | critical |
| accepting | accepting |
| | |
| **Goals** | **Goals** |
| short and long-term | short and long-term |
| being successful in business | getting married |
| getting season football tickets | finishing school |
| finding the right girl | having children |
| | |

## Short Personality Template

| Male | Female |
|---|---|
| Age | Age |
| Superficial attributes | Superficial attributes |
| looks and personality | looks and personality |
|  |  |
| Sexual interests | Sexual interests |
| Interests | Interests |
| activities/hobbies | activities/hobbies |
|  |  |
| Pet peeves | Pet peeves |
|  |  |
| Strengths & weaknesses | Strengths & weaknesses |
|  |  |
| Level of responsibility | Level of responsibility |
|  |  |
| Interactive skills | Interactive skills |
| compromise/insightful | compromise/insightful |
|  |  |
| Marriage | Marriage |
| time together | time together |
|  |  |
| Financial security | Financial security |
|  |  |
| Children | Children |
| quality of interaction | quality of interaction |
|  |  |
| Goals | Goals |
| short and long-term | short and long-term |

## Husband-Wife-Significant Other
## Template

| Male/Female | Female/Male |
|---|---|
| **Husband** | **Wife** |
| **Age** | **Age** |
| **Interactions** | **Interactions** |
| caring/distant | caring/distant |
| individual time | individual time |
| | |
| time together | time together |
| | |
| communicative | communicative |
| open and honest/sharing | open and honest/sharing |
| movie/dining out together | movie/dining out together |
| | |
| **Sexual behaviors** | **Sexual behaviors** |
| | |
| **Financial security** | **Financial security** |
| job stability | job stability |
| good income | good income |
| | |
| **Children** | **Children** |
| wanted? | wanted? |
| cares for/dislikes? | cares for/dislikes? |
| family eats together | family eats together |
| | |
| spends time with them | spends time with them |
| answers their questions | answers their questions |

| | |
|---|---|
| takes them places | takes them places |
| takes them on vacations | takes them on vacations |
| goes to school programs | goes to school programs |
| limits TV/video time | limits TV/video time |
| | |
| **Goals** | **Goals** |
| short and long-term | short and long-term |
| building a pension | buying a house |
| saving money | getting the kids into college |
| | |

# Boss – Manager Template

| Boss | You |
|---|---|
| **Male or female** | is that a problem? |
| **Age** | **Age** |
| **Type of industry** | |
| **Superficial attributes** | |
| grooming-attire | do you like him? |
| isolates | |
| works with employees | |
| irritable and critical | |
| well respected | |
| hated | |
| productivity at any cost | |
| | |
| **Personal interests** | |
| keeps to himself | |
| well-known to employees | |
| | |
| **Strengths & weaknesses** | |
| smart | |
| common sense | |
| peculiarities? | |
| predictable | |
| can hold a grudge | |
| alcoholic? | |
| open to new ideas | |
| **Goals** | |
| maximize profits | can you work with him? |
| employee participation in benefits | |

## Male & Female Personality Differences Template

| Male | Female |
|---|---|
| TV-football/sports in general | shopping |
| golfing | shoe shopping |
| fishing | crafts |
| boating | cooking |
| physically more powerful | manicures |
| short-term pleasures | cosmetics/perfumes |
| | hairstyling |
| | spas |
| | classical music |
| | opera |
| | long-term goals |
| | |

# Personality Template

| Male | Female |
|---|---|
| **Age** | **Age** |
| **Significant family background** | **Significant family background** |
|  |  |
| **Superficial attributes** | **Superficial attributes** |
| looks-handsome | looks-beautiful |
| attire-well groomed/sloppy | attire-well groomed/sloppy |
| casual ?/stylish | casual?/stylish |
| energetic | energetic |
| sociable | sociable |
| quiet | quiet |
| polite/offensive | polite/offensive |
| serious/sense of humor | serious/sense of humor |
|  |  |
| **Sexual interests** | **Sexual interests** |
| sexual frequency/interest | sexual frequency/interest |
| sexual capacity | sexual capacity |
| promiscuous | promiscuous |
|  |  |
| **Interests** | **Interests** |
| movies | movies |
| sports | sports |
| music | music |
| traveling | traveling |
| dining out | dining out |
| cultural events/museums | cultural events/museums |
|  |  |

| Vacation preferences | Vacation preferences |
|---|---|
| travel | travel |
| skiing | skiing |
| casino visiting | casino visiting |
| cruises | cruises |
| seashore activities | seashore activities |
| | |
| **Hobbies** | **Hobbies** |
| crafts | woodworking |
| pets | car models |
| | |
| **Pet peeves** | **Pet peeves** |
| washing dishes | washing dishes |
| being nagged | washing clothes |
| going to work | ironing |
| | procrastinating |
| | |
| **Strengths & weaknesses** | **Strengths & weaknesses** |
| basic intelligence-IQ | basic intelligence-IQ |
| educational level | educational level |
| common sense | common sense |
| neurotic? | neurotic |
| peculiarity? | peculiarity? |
| | |
| responsibility | responsibility |
| family | family |
| job-employment | job-employment |
| financial | financial |
| saves/spendthrift | saves/spendthrift |

| | |
|---|---|
| drug & alcohol addiction | drug & alcohol addiction |
| religious preference | religious preference |
| prejudices | prejudices |
| | |
| selfish/caring | selfish/caring |
| **Interactive skills** | **Interactive skills** |
| ability to compromise | ability to compromise |
| introspective/insightful | introspective/insightful |
| dogmatic | dogmatic |
| critical | critical |
| accepting | accepting |
| | |
| **Goals** | **Goals** |
| short and long-term | short and long-term |
| being successful in business | getting married |
| getting season football tickets | finishing school |
| finding the right girl | having children |
| | |

## Short Personality Template

| Male | Female |
|---|---|
| Age | Age |
| Superficial attributes | Superficial attributes |
| looks and personality | looks and personality |
| | |
| Sexual interests | Sexual interests |
| Interests | Interests |
| activities/hobbies | activities/hobbies |
| | |
| Pet peeves | Pet peeves |
| | |
| Strengths & weaknesses | Strengths & weaknesses |
| | |
| Level of responsibility | Level of responsibility |
| | |
| Interactive skills | Interactive skills |
| compromise/insightful | compromise/insightful |
| | |
| Marriage | Marriage |
| time together | time together |
| | |
| Financial security | Financial security |
| | |
| Children | Children |
| quality of interaction | quality of interaction |
| | |
| Goals | Goals |
| short and long-term | short and long-term |

## Husband-Wife-Significant Other
## Template

| Male/Female | Female/Male |
|---|---|
| Husband | Wife |
| Age | Age |
| Interactions | Interactions |
| caring/distant | caring/distant |
| individual time | individual time |
| | |
| time together | time together |
| | |
| communicative | communicative |
| open and honest/sharing | open and honest/sharing |
| movie/dining out together | movie/dining out together |
| | |
| Sexual behaviors | Sexual behaviors |
| | |
| Financial security | Financial security |
| job stability | job stability |
| good income | good income |
| | |
| Children | Children |
| wanted? | wanted? |
| cares for/dislikes? | cares for/dislikes? |
| family eats together | family eats together |
| | |
| spends time with them | spends time with them |
| answers their questions | answers their questions |

| | |
|---|---|
| takes them places | takes them places |
| takes them on vacations | takes them on vacations |
| goes to school programs | goes to school programs |
| limits TV/video time | limits TV/video time |
| | |
| **Goals** | **Goals** |
| short and long-term | short and long-term |
| building a pension | buying a house |
| saving money | getting the kids into college |
| | |

## Boss – Manager Template

| Boss | You |
|---|---|
| **Male or female** | is that a problem? |
| **Age** | **Age** |
| **Type of industry** | |
| **Superficial attributes** | |
| grooming-attire | do you like him? |
| isolates | |
| works with employees | |
| irritable and critical | |
| well respected | |
| hated | |
| productivity at any cost | |
| | |
| **Personal interests** | |
| keeps to himself | |
| well-known to employees | |
| | |
| **Strengths & weaknesses** | |
| smart | |
| common sense | |
| peculiarities? | |
| predictable | |
| can hold a grudge | |
| alcoholic? | |
| open to new ideas | |
| **Goals** | |
| maximize profits | can you work with him? |
| employee participation in benefits | |

www.ingramcontent.com/pod-product-compliance
Lightning Source LLC
Chambersburg PA
CBHW060433290526
45791CB00002B/938